The Great American Fourth of July Parade

Bicentennial Selection
of the International Poetry Forum

Works by Archibald MacLeish

Poems

Collected Poems, 1917–1952

 including The Hamlet of A. MacLeish, Conquistador, Streets in the Moon, New Found Land, Public Speech, Actfive, and others

Songs for Eve

Wild Old Wicked Man

The Human Season: Selected Poems, 1926–1972

Plays in Verse

Panic

This Music Crept by Me upon the Waters

J. B.

Herakles

Verse Plays for Radio

The Fall of the City

Air Raid

The Trojan Horse

The Great American Fourth of July Parade

Play in Prose

Scratch

Prose Collections

The Irresponsibles

A Time to Speak

A Time to Act

Freedom Is the Right to Choose

Poetry and Experience

A Continuing Journey

THE GREAT AMERICAN

FOURTH OF JULY PARADE

A Verse Play for Radio

Archibald MacLeish

University of Pittsburgh Press

First printing 1975
Paperback reissue 1976

Library of Congress Catalog Card Number 74—24682
ISBN 0—8229—3300—4 (cloth)
ISBN 0—8229—5272—6 (paper)

*Publication of this book
has been made possible
by grants to the International
Poetry Forum and the University
of Pittsburgh Press from
the A. W. Mellon Educational
and Charitable Trust.*

The Great American Fourth of July Parade

DIRECTOR

(*broadcasting voice*)

Stand by, ladies and gentlemen . . .

(*headphone voice: to his engineers*)

Quiet! We're on the air.

(*pause: inaudible reply*)

Who'd be standing by at four A.M.?
I'll tell you, laddie. All New England.
All New England in the waiting night.

(*pause*)

Yes, *waiting!*

      For the daylight!

            For the great

two hundredth anniversary!

(*pause*)

          Of what?

Liberty they used to call it.

(*pause*)

Human liberty! You heard me.

(*pause*)

Say that on your own time, mate, and not to
me!

Archibald MacLeish

Let's get on with it. Page one.

(*reading*)

"Every church bell in New England ringing."

(*carillon of synthetic chimes*)

That's what church bells sound like in New England
now? Electronic doorbells?
Back a generation you could hear them swing:
men pulled ropes when bells were rung.
What rings them these days? A transistor?

(*The carillon breaks off awkwardly. Silence. A deep, slow bell*)

                                        No!

I tell you No! But *no*. The one thing
church bells in New England never were
is what that sounds like, if you get me.
Think of a country steeple under country stars.
Think of an old man in a kind of closet.
He has a rope's end in his hands.
It's dark. A light bulb. Lantern maybe.
The church smells empty as an attic, old
as floorboards in a sagging barn.
There's nobody awake for miles—he knows that:
only, off beyond him somewhere,
deeper in the night, the hills,
a bell that answers his bell answering.

The rope pulls. The reverberating iron
rings. He hears that other ringing. Conway
answering Chocorua. Which answers.

Think of that closet and the slender rope
worn smooth with human hands for generations—
with human handling. That's New England—
church bells in New England—steeple
answering to steeple in New England.

(*The deep bell dims and dies: there is a faint far clanging back and
forth.*)

That's better. That's more like it. Now
ring them will you? Let them *ring!*
This is *their* anniversary, remember?

(*a rising surge of sound: an iron cadence*)

Yes but louder, louder, louder:
Jubilation of rejoicing bells!
Rejoicing bells!

(*a great surge, a singing cadence*)

        All New England
ringing-in the holy dawn!
Every trembling steeple in New England
clear from Deerfield down to Bangor, Maine;
south to Connecticut; New Haven Green;

Farmington, that slender silver;
Saybrook east to Falmouth; Boston;
Marblehead; Cape Ann, Cape Ann;
Nantucket where the bells are buoys;
Provincetown across the water . . .

That rings it! Out and in! The second century
gone beyond the Alleghenies,
the third new risen off the coast of Maine.
"Fare well!" the bells say westward, "Oh, farewell!"
"Well come!" they say to eastward, "Welcome!"

Aye, *listen* to them!

(*crescendo of the singing iron*)

                No, but *listen!*

(*The cadence cracks, breaks, tumbles into a sudden counterrhythm
not of bells.*)
                      Something
under . . .
        like a drum beat . . .
                heart beat . . .
frantic heart beat . . .
            stumbling drums . . .
(*pause*)

What do you mean you can't hear anything?

You have to hear it. Hurrying footfall.
Multitudes along the thronging streets.
You're picking up the thud of panic—
racing feet of fear . . .

(*pause*)

                How should *I* know!
How should I know what they fear?
Maybe the bells have terrified them.
Maybe what the bells foretell.

(*pause*)

             Foretell!

(*pause*)

Do? What *can* you do? Immense antennae
probing through the pulses of the night
are bound to pick up something in a time like this one—
panic footsteps or those short-wave voices,
veering through the frequencies, that speak
where no voice should speak, or not theirs.
You have your masts up and your nets are rigged
to catch the whispering world and you can't stop it.
I can't stop it. Nothing we can do but
keep the channels open and go on—
let the script go on—and listen.

Listen:

Archibald MacLeish

"Down east in Maine
the sky is brightening where it meets the water.
Massachusetts is still dark.
Virginia is deep in darkness . . ."

So! We're deep in darkness. In Virginia.
"Summer leaves," it says. "A dog off somewhere."
Let's hear the summer leaves, the dog.

(*a distant barking: night wind in night leaves*)

Midsummer wind . . .

                    midsummer trees . . .

(*an old man's dry cough nearer than the wind sound*)

Ha!

(*violin strings plucked to tune them*)

    That wasn't? . . .

(*crash of a bow on the strings: shout of laughter*)

           No, it wasn't *you.*

O L D   M A N ' S   V O I C E
(*Virginian but not our kind of Virginian*)

Listen to this, John Adams! Listen!

(*a high, exultant tune, not well played, badly either*)

Hear?

8

(*silence*)

Well, you will hear.

(*the tune again, triumphant. Silence*)

DIRECTOR

Voices
veering through the frequencies that speak
where no voice should speak . . .

What I told you.

OLD MAN'S VOICE

I do not take your
silence kindly, Mister Adams . . .

DIRECTOR

You can't stop it. I can't stop it.
I'll be here if you need me . . . listening!

OLD MAN'S VOICE

It must be almost morning in the Massachusetts—
almost day. You know what day, sir!

(*silence: the wind*)

I said, you know what day.

Archibald MacLeish

(*silence: the lapsing leaves*)

                    This!

(*crash of the bow on the strings: the theme of the triumphant tune,
harsh and fierce as the blast of a trumpet*)

The Fourth of July, Mister Adams!

                              The Fourth of July!

The glorious anniversary of the famous day
when you and I and all that host of worthies
gathered in Philadelphia in the thronging room,
annulled the ancient bondage of humanity—
changed the world . . .

(*silence*)

                    You do not hear me even

now?—even remembering what we remember?

(*silence*)

I said I do not take your silence
kindly, Mister Adams. It was you, not I,
after the lifetime of our love and hate,
wrote that adjuration: "We ought not to die
before we had explained ourselves to one another."
I kept that charge at heart and I obeyed you—
fourteen years of letters back and forth—
and when you made an end of it, I ended:
we two together on the selfsame day.

10

(*silence*)

We learned to love each other, Mister Adams,
learning to love our country as we did.
We made its anniversary our own but now—
now that the day comes round again,
now that the second century is over,
the third begins, you will not speak nor hear.

A D A M S

(*a Yankee voice creaking with time like an autumn cricket*)

Oh, I hear you . . .

(*preoccupied*)

                I hear you, Mister Jefferson . . .

(*pause*)

But there is something else I also hear . . .

J E F F E R S O N

You mean the fiddler and his fiddle?

A D A M S

I love the fiddler—he knows that.
As for the fiddle, I can tolerate it.
It's what I hear beneath that strikes me dumb.

JEFFERSON

The music? But that's Beethoven himself.
The great new man. Beethoven. His *Eroica*.

ADAMS

The piece he dedicated to that rogue, Napoleon.

JEFFERSON

Undedicated when Napoleon took the crown.

ADAMS

Who was his hero *then?*

JEFFERSON

                    Mankind.

ADAMS

What you called "all men" in your famous Declaration—
"all men are created equal."
You shared a hero in the end, you two.
But where your new composer's Bonaparte
left him with a *dédicace* to blot,
your "all men" never once embarrassed you.
They took to history like Hector to his fable
launched as they were on your immortal lines.

JEFFERSON

Laugh at me as you please, sir, but that Declaration
bears your signature as well as mine.
What did *you* mean, Mister Adams?

ADAMS

Mean? I meant an end to kings!
To men who act like kings! To men
pretending by the chance of rule
to master other men, manipulate them,
lie to them, deceive, degrade . . .

JEFFERSON

Canker their equal rights as equal men!

ADAMS

You are our philosopher, Mister Jefferson.
Men, to my mind, are created men, not
equal, and must make the best of it—
rulers and ruled. I meant a country
cleansed of arrogance where human kind
is all the kind there is—a country,
open and honest, where the people need not fear.

JEFFERSON

Fear what?

A D A M S

    Fear for their country. For its future.

J E F F E R S O N

Fear? In *this* Republic? For *our* future?

A D A M S

I've heard the fear. I've listened to it.

J E F F E R S O N

                         Not on

this day!

A D A M S

    On this *day*. This morning.
All night long since midnight when the Quincy bells
counted the last slow seconds of that century
I've heard a kind of distant drumming,
a terrified heartbeat . . .

J E F F E R S O N

                 No. The beat of
jubilation—festival: the quickening rhythm . . .

A D A M S

And after it a stir upon the earth,

a gathering multitude, a thronging
rumor on the country roads.

JEFFERSON

The thronging of delighted men and women
pressing toward morning, toward the new, bright day.

ADAMS

By night. In silence. Stumbling through the night.

JEFFERSON

Silence is not fear, my troubled friend.
Expectation has its silences as well—
its catching of the breath. Their souls
expect the celebration of their triumph.

ADAMS

You do not hear them, Mister Jefferson. I hear them . . .

(*the hurrying sound*)

. . . and what I hear is faltering, uncertain
footsteps on the roads, the lanes,
the woodlands even, like a wakened people
driven from some great city by a voice
over the housetops in the darkness crying
ruin—crying that the nations fall—
that even the greatest nations of mankind have fallen.

Archibald MacLeish

JEFFERSON

Not the American nation, Mister Adams.
No possible generation of Americans
is capable of that disastrous fear.
We do not dread our destiny in America.
Remember how the whole of Europe laughed at us?—
our cheerful confidence in God, in life, in
everything on earth or out of it?

A sovereign people never can despair.

ADAMS

Even a sovereign people that's no longer sovereign?
Even a sovereign people that has learned
its servants have become its masters?
That those who govern, govern for themselves?
A knave in office and a palace guard of fools?

JEFFERSON

Ah, Mister Adams, Mister Adams.
You told me once you had a malady
nothing but the earth could cure.
I know now what it was—your tongue.
And Quincy church loam has not cured it—
even that granite crypt in Quincy ground.

ADAMS

While you, my friend, although you had no maladies—
teeth still sound at eighty, eyes

keen as a rifleman's when all the rest were
blind or going on for blindness—
you, without a malady, are much,
much altered in the tomb. That famous
president whose famous tombstone
makes no mention of the presidential office—
"Father of the University of Virginia,"
"Author of the Declaration," yes,
but president of the United States?
No word to say so. Where is he?
Where is that homespun citizen, that country
cousin who preferred the plow to
office and philosophy to fame?
Where is he now? Where's Thomas Jefferson?
Up before dawn to tune his fiddle,
wake his country for the festival parade,
the national anniversary . . .

                              Those ears
that still hear orioles and skylarks,
deaf to the panic pounding in the blood!

JEFFERSON

This is no "national anniversary," Mister Adams.
This is the anniversary of that remembered day
when we, protagonists to humanity, declared
the bold new purpose of mankind:

to lick the spittle of presumptuous kings
no longer from our cheeks—to rule ourselves.
And we did rule ourselves. And these Americans
thronging to the celebration of their century
know it as well as I do—well as you.
You were at Philadelphia, John Adams!
You were at Philadelphia in that stifling room,
the rumbling of the carts across the cobbles,
thunder beyond the Schuylkill. You were there.
You answered Dickinson of Pennsylvania.
You moved the Congress with its thirteen minds,
innumerable voices. And you saved the cause.

A D A M S
Beloved adversary!

J E F F E R S O N
                    Cantankerous friend!
You cannot doubt the greatness of that great decision.
You were the center of the crowded room
where men stood staring at each other and their destiny—
their country's indecipherable fate . . . humanity's!

(*pause*)

now no longer indecipherable:
now proven by two hundred years.

ADAMS

Not proven for those throngs along the highways—
that gathering dread.

JEFFERSON

Gathering dread!
Oh, you Yankees! You incredulous Yankees!
You will not let yourselves believe in triumph
even with triumph in your hands—a multitude
pouring in to celebrate it—
crown your labors with its praise, inscribe your
names in marble and repeat your sayings,
even the glorious sayings that you never said.
What do they feed their children in the Massachusetts?
Mushrooms? Edible at peril?

ADAMS

I believe my ears,
not what I hope my ears will tell me.
It is not triumph that I hear—not praise or
gratitude or celebration . . .

(*thud of footsteps on the earth: the hurrying sound nearer and
nearer*)

It is fear.

(*The sound breaks suddenly off. Silence. Dead silence*)

Archibald MacLeish

JEFFERSON

You mean you . . . hear them still?

ADAMS

I did hear them.

JEFFERSON

You thought you heard them and they've gone.

ADAMS

Stopped, not gone. Beneath the granite
sounds are deafened. I could hear them come
hurrying nearer—then not hurrying.
I think they stand there now on Quincy Common—
what was once the Quincy Common—
bandstand for the festival occasions,
bunting underneath the elms.
God knows what it looks like these days.

JEFFERSON

I doubt the Deity records such matters.
What they've come for, though, is evident enough.
They've come to you, sir. To salute you.
Honor you on your day of days.

ADAMS

More likely for the comfort of remembrance:
a relic of the past to reassure them—

maybe the balm of a familiar word
they hope some orator will button round their souls.
They need the past to bolster their poor present up,
quiet their apprehensions, prove
the great Republic once *was* great Republic . . .

Yes, they're there. I hear them standing still
the way a horse stands still . . . and trembles.

JEFFERSON

                                        Why do you
rail against your countrymen, Mister Adams?
They come to do you honor—speak your name.

ADAMS
No, sir. They come for refuge from their lives
or from their country's life or what
they think corrupts their country—has corrupted it.
They think the sky is falling and they ask for shelter—
something more substantial than that monument of yours,
that up-thrust finger pointing past the stars
at human liberty. The frightened
have no time for human liberty.
What they ask is cover overhead—
a solid Yankee slab of Yankee granite.

(*a brass band: a Sousa tootle of cheerful trombones, rattling drums*)

JEFFERSON

You wrong them and yourself. They stand there
breathless in their love for you,
their gratitude for what you gave them:
freedom not from England but from kings,
all kings, all masters. They have come
to celebrate that freedom on its anniversary—
hear the words that celebrate it—hear
the sentences two hundred years remember:
our sentences: our promise to mankind.

(*The band breaks off.*)

ADAMS

Well, sir . . .

(*a chuckle*)

                    whatever they expect to hear
may God be with them now. The orator has risen.

BULLHORN VOICE

Ladies and gentlemen! Ladies and gentlemen!
Pray silence for the Honorable . . .

ADAMS

Honorable somebody—I couldn't hear.
Some dignitary from the capital in Washington.

You'll hear him far as Monticello—
the usual sentiments of course—
a word for me as tutelary saint—
a word for you as author of the document—
more extended words for General Washington.
Fortunately none of us can blush . . .

ORATOR

(oritund, amplified, politician voice)

Thank you!

       Thank you!

ADAMS

       Here he goes . . .

ORATOR

I have one thing to say to you, my fellow Americans . . .

(He clears his throat. Professional pause)

One thing.

JEFFERSON

       Right so far at least.

ORATOR

One thing you must never for a single moment,
least of all this greatest, this most glorious moment,

this solemn ceremony of the year . . .

(*applause*)

I say the year. I mean the century . . .

(*applause*)

Nay, I mean the second century . . .

(*louder applause*)

J E F F E R S O N
The second century, Mister Adams!

O R A T O R

One

thing . . .

A D A M S

Well, get on with it! Get on with it . . .

O R A T O R
One thing you must never, while you live and breathe,
whatever else excites your interest,
whatever else concerns your thought . . .

J E F F E R S O N
Give him time: he's coming to it.

ORATOR

One thing you must never, while you live, forget:
The U.S.A., my fellow Americans . . .

ADAMS

He refers to the Republic.

ORATOR

The U.S.A., my fellow Americans . . .
The U.S.A. . . . .

(*anticipatory pause: the thunder of expected cheers gathering behind it*)

IS NUMBER ONE!

(*silence—dead silence*)

JEFFERSON

Not, it seems, the kind of reassurance
even a frightened people welcomes.

ORATOR

(*rattled: a nasty edge to his voice*)

And I have one more thing to say!
Never forget it yourselves and never,
never while you breathe and live,
let anyone else on earth forget it!

(*pause*)

Will your admirable buglers rise?
We need the emphasis of music. Thank you.

(*shattering amplification*)

THE U.S.A. IS NUMBER ONE!

(*the bugles: ta-ta-ta-TAAA!*)
(*the whole band: ta-ta-ta-TAAAAAA!*)
(*silence*)

A D A M S

Not one answering handclap. Not a sound.

J E F F E R S O N

Conceivably they think there's something more to say . . .
or should be.

A D A M S

                Not a sound. As still
as summer pasture when the quiet turf
waits for grazing cattle . . .
                     No,
listen! There's someone striding off—
an old man by the step, perhaps a
veteran of forgotten wars—
a lighter, quicker step behind him—
others after them—still others—
a family with little children . . .

JEFFERSON

Veterans of wars; their wives,

stooping their proud, white heads; their children . . .

You said these marchers in the night were frightened.

You said a listener could tell their fear

hearing their feet upon the earth. I think the

word is anger, sir. I think you

know the word is anger . . .

ORATOR

(*shouting*)

                              Look at them

go! Look at them run for it! Look at them!

Sure, there are other countries on the earth:

go off and find one if you have a mind to!

Only let me tell you this:

Never in your farthest journey,

never in the widest world,

will any one of you find wealth like our wealth,

power like ours, wealth and power.

More Americans eat more meat!

More Americans use more shoes!

More Americans live more life!

There are more millionaires per mile in America!

More millionaires per mile in America!

(*the band in an ecstasy of jazzing brass*)

Archibald MacLeish

ADAMS

Now there are crowds of them stalking off.

ORATOR

(*outshouting the band*)

And let me say this to you. Let me say this.
We have peace in the world at last—at least
American peace: peace for Americans.
Why? Because we have the power.
Why? Because we have the missiles.
Why? Because we have the kill.
We have more kill per missile in America!
We have more kill per missile in America!
We have more kill per missile in America
than anywhere else beneath the blazing sun.

(*The band, breathless, breaks off. The Orator's voice goes on, matter-of-fact, unamplified, almost gentle.*)

The U.S.A. is number one.

(*silence: then an hysterical yell*)

THE U.S.A. IS NUMBER ONE!

(*stunned silence*)

You can like it or not, my friends . . . if you are.
If not—if not it doesn't matter:
the U.S.A. will still be number one.

ADAMS

That must be the end of it. Someone claps . . .
thinks better of it . . .

(*faint sound of applause*)

       Awkward moment—
awkward for a politician.
Embarrassed aides . . . the local committee
mumbling something unintelligible . . .
most of the rest gone off or simply dumb . . .

LITTLE GIRL

I want to see the U.S.A.

SECOND LITTLE GIRL

We can't *see* the U.S.A.

BULLHORN VOICE

Fall in, ladies and gentlemen.

ADAMS

There's the marshal marshaling his parade.

BULLHORN VOICE

Fall in! Take your places!

ADAMS

Not a word from the distinguished orator.

SECOND LITTLE GIRL

Nobody has seen the U.S.A.

LITTLE GIRL

My grandfather saw it.

SECOND LITTLE GIRL

            Where?

LITTLE GIRL

                    In France.

SECOND LITTLE GIRL

He couldn't in France.

LITTLE GIRL

            He did. He told me.
He was in France in the Great War
and they stood retreat in a field and he saw it.
He cried.

SECOND LITTLE GIRL

      Why?

LITTLE GIRL

            I don't know.
The bugle blew at sunset and he saw it.

SECOND LITTLE GIRL

I've never seen it.

LITTLE GIRL

Neither have I.

(*pause: the bullhorn voice beyond*)

JEFFERSON

And that's the celebration of the anniversary . . . ?

ADAMS

. . . of your immortal Declaration!

JEFFERSON

Do not
laugh at me, old friend.

ADAMS

I've never laughed at you.
Raged? Oh, yes I've raged, but never
once in all our bouts and battles have I laughed.
You had a look that did not tempt to laughter.

JEFFERSON

You should have! More than once and never
louder or more scornfully than now.
I said those midnight marchers came

Archibald MacLeish

to celebrate the anniversary of freedom.
You should have howled with laughter, Mister Adams.
You knew they came for syrups for their fears.
The great two hundredth year, the second century,
celebrated with those brags of wealth, of power!

A D A M S
Not them: they wouldn't listen to it.

B U L L H O R N   V O I C E
Fall in! Fall in!

J E F F E R S O N
No, and neither will they march.

A D A M S
Not for him, perhaps. If Mister Jefferson . . .

J E F F E R S O N
Mister Jefferson. *Mister* Jefferson!
They have no stomach for a cause like Mister Jefferson's.
Your guess was right, sir: they are frightened.

A D A M S
You used to tell me, Mister Jefferson,
I did not trust the people as I should.
Now it is you who do not trust them.

32

After those revelations of the rot at heart,
the rank corruption of the soul,
how can they help but fear? The greatest
nations of the earth have perished
not of their enemies but of themselves—
their souls. They know that. And they fear it.

JEFFERSON

We also feared but we believed—
thrust our necks into the noose of treason,
fought our barefoot war . . .

ADAMS

                              Remind them!

JEFFERSON

. . . fought our barefoot war! And why?
Because we had a cause to fight for.
They have no cause but comfort—but security.

ADAMS

Then talk to them, Mister Jefferson. If someone—
someone *they* believed—would talk to them . . .

BULLHORN VOICE

                                        Fall
in!

Archibald MacLeish

ADAMS

There must be marching on the Fourth July.
There must be ceremony, pomp, parade,
sports, games, shows, guns,
bonfires and illuminations.
Men must remember, this day, who they are
or what they are will leave them. Pride and
purpose must go marching on this day.

BULLHORN VOICE

Fall in! *Fall in!*

ADAMS

Tell them, Mister Jefferson.

JEFFERSON

                        They would not
listen to me if I did.

ADAMS

              The whole,
great world has listened to you, Mister Jefferson!

JEFFERSON

Long ago! Who listens to a dead man?

ADAMS

The living—when his words still live.
You are remembered, Mister Jefferson.

JEFFERSON

Remembered but not believed.

ADAMS

                              Contemptuous voices
jeering in the dark declare
the journey of mankind is ended:
the truth, they say, is out now—we are naked apes,
disgusting animals, ignoble creatures.
But when they say this they remember you
and some few others on the road beside
who put their trust where you did—in humanity.
They ask each other how those victories were won
that now, without a gunshot, are surrendered . . .

and they think of you.

JEFFERSON

                         They should be thinking
not of me or you or any of us. They shoud be
thinking how their country came to be—
what called it out of nothing in a wilderness.
The word that called it.

ADAMS

                         The great act
of independence.

JEFFERSON

                    Revolution, Mister Adams.

We, in our time, called it revolution.

Now they've forgotten what the revolution was.

ADAMS

Our separation from the British crown.

JEFFERSON

Much more than that. Much more than that.

Read the writ again, sir. Read

"the causes which impelled that separation . . ."

We spelled them out for all the world to see:

they were the causes of all men—mankind.

ADAMS

Those were the reasons afterward: not the causes.

JEFFERSON

Reasons that live afterward become the causes.

Do not deny your triumph, Mister Adams.

I see you standing in the stifling room

speaking "separation from the British crown"

in words that rang the revolution of humanity.

We struck that bell, sir. It was we,

laboring through that summer for a common ground

capable of our republic, who first struck it,

started the metal singing, felled the kings
like crows across the continent of Europe . . .

ADAMS

And filled their thrones with what? Gray, faceless
despots worse than any king.

JEFFERSON

Because we had abandoned our great bell—
left it to other-minded men
to ring for other purposes—their own . . .

(*pause*)

You and I first quarreled on this question.

ADAMS

First and last.

JEFFERSON

　　　　No. At the last I wrote a letter
not to you but to the citizens of Washington
telling them what our Declaration was—
what I believed it was. You never read it.
You and I were gone when it saw print.

(*pause*)

Shall I tell you what that letter said—

you and your midnight marchers? . . .

　　　　　　　　　　　If they'll listen?

A D A M S

We'd have no choice but listen, any of us.
Letters or violins, if Thomas Jefferson
starts the music all men listen.

J E F F E R S O N

　　　　　　　Violins!

(*crash of the bow across the fiddle strings: the first few notes of the
now familiar theme*)

Fellow citizens! . . .

(*silence*)

　　　　　　　. . . of the Great Republic! . . .

Can you hear me, fellow citizens?

A D A M S

They stand there motionless—no sound:
only their stillness on the stones, the grasses . . .

J E F F E R S O N

People of the Great Republic! . . .

(*Voices—contemporary—some old, some young—bitter and ironic,
some of them—tired and despairing, others. A few with thoughts on
this or that—a schoolmarm—a bright student. One—a sweet young
thing—with words*)

OLD MAN

There's someone calling to us somewhere . . .

WOMAN

Somewhere else, it sounds like . . .

OLD MAN

                              Not
near or far but somewhere else . . .

JEFFERSON

I have a tale to tell you, fellow citizens:
a tale of many, many years ago—
the fiftieth anniversary of the Republic.

(*pause: silence*)

I was in Monticello in that summer—
ill . . .

        an old man . . .

                        destitute . . .
(*pause*)

dying as the thing turned out . . .

WOMAN

He says he died at Monticello.
That's in Virginia where Thomas Jefferson . . .

Archibald MacLeish

O L D   M A N

Thomas Jefferson is dead. Long dead.

S C H O O L M A R M

He certainly is. Long since dead.
He died on the fiftieth Fourth July at
noon—forenoon.

W O M A N

The *Fourth July!*

S C H O O L M A R M

Call that curious I'll tell you queer.
It wasn't only him that died that Fourth.
John Adams, his inveterate opponent,
dearest friend, died too. In Massachusetts.
They called the folks in 'long 'bout four.
"Thomas Jefferson survives," he told 'em.
Seemed contented and just turned away.

There was a story told the smell of clover
drifted through the room—the late-cut hay.

S W E E T   Y O U N G   T H I N G

Patriotic sentimental . . .

S C H O O L M A R M

Every meetinghouse and church in all America,

people gathered. Those two dying,
both together, on the Fourth July,
the fiftieth Fourth July, they thought
a witness had been given them—a sign from
God for the Republic . . .

SWEET YOUNG THING

Shit!

JEFFERSON

I was in Monticello in that summer.
There was a letter came from the city of Washington
"to the surviving signers of an instrument
pregnant with fate, their own and the world's."

BRIGHT BOY

What's an instrument?

SCHOOLMARM

A writing.

BRIGHT BOY

I know what it was: the Declaration.
To the surviving signers of the Declaration.
Thomas Jefferson was a signer of the Declaration.

YOUNG MAN

Thomas Jefferson was a *signer!*

Archibald MacLeish

Thomas Jefferson *wrote* those noble sentiments!
"All men are created equal."

Y O U N G   M A N
And it's true. It's come true. Look at the
Blacks! They're *all* equal.

Y O U N G   M A N
And it's true too what he wrote about happiness.
Every word of it's come true.
We have the right from Thomas Jefferson to pursue it.
Watch the poor damn hungry Indians pursuing!
Read the advertisements and pursue—pursue!

J E F F E R S O N
There was a letter came from the city of Washington—
an invitation to attend
the jubilee of that immortal instrument.
I could not go.

A D A M S
                    Nor I.

(*his chuckling laugh*)

                    Nor I.
We were expected, as you might say, elsewhere.

42

JEFFERSON

And so I wrote a letter to the people. I told them, "I should indeed
with peculiar delight have met with the small band, the remnant of
the host of worthies who joined that day in the bold and doubtful
election we were to make for our country . . ."

BRIGHT BOY

What does he mean, "the bold and doubtful election"?

YOUNG MAN

Independence. Liberty. *You* know:
what all men have a right to—

                    nothing!

YOUNG MAN

Like when you're free to believe what the government says to you.

YOUNG MAN

What the public relations punks in the government say to you.

BRIGHT BOY

But the government *has* to tell the truth.
It says in the Declaration of Independence . . .

YOUNG MAN

Don't tell me . . .

Archibald MacLeish

B R I G H T   B O Y

   . . . that governments derive their powers . . .

S C H O O L M A R M

Their *just* powers!

B R I G H T   B O Y

   . . . from the governed.

S C H O O L M A R M

The *consent* of the governed.

B R I G H T   B O Y

   Consent of the governed.

Y O U N G   M A N

   So?

B R I G H T   B O Y

So how can the governed consent if they don't know?

Y O U N G   M A N

You mean if they aren't told? If their government lies to them?
Good question, boy. They can't.

B R I G H T   B O Y

So what becomes of the powers of government?

44

YOUNG MAN

Nothing at all. The government keeps them.
The question is, What happens to the Declaration?

SWEET YOUNG THING

I know what happens to the Declaration. You can . . .

YOUNG MAN

The Declaration is so much laundered crap.
Poopsy Cola. Public relations.

YOUNG MAN

Like everything else in the goddam country.

WOMAN

All men are created equal . . .
Maybe! But government is run by someone else.

OLD MAN

For someone else.

OLD WOMAN

         By other methods:
by private secrets and by public lies.

YOUNG MAN

By the FBI at night with its ears to the telephones.

Archibald MacLeish

SWEET YOUNG THING

Nobody gives a damn about the Declaration.

Nobody ever gave a damn about it.

All those sucking saps endowed by their creator . . .

YOUNG MAN

Endowed with those unalienable rights

nobody respects and honors!

OLD MAN

Even Thomas Jefferson himself—

you think he meant that crap—that Declaration?

JEFFERSON

"May it be to the world," I wrote to the people of Washington,

"what I believe it will be: to some parts sooner, to others later, but

finally to all . . ."

YOUNG MAN

"May it be to the world!" To the world! The *world!*

Why should the world have noticed even?

Noticed the words—ridiculous rhetoric?

Noticed the war—the poor damn war—

that Lexington hayfield where the farmers stood,

a dozen dead, a couple dozen wounded—

how could all that matter to the world?

GIRL

I don't know. You can't be certain.
Maybe something started in that hayfield—
something the world had never seen before.
Maybe the Declaration was a kind of matchstick,
a kindling in the winter hay,
even the whole wide world would have to notice.

JEFFERSON

"May it be to the world what I believe it will be . . . the signal of
arousing men to burst the chains . . ."

YOUNG MAN

What does he mean, arousing men?
He was a Southern planter wasn't he?
Owned slaves? He could have freed them.

BLACK GIRL

Maybe he thought his Declaration,
once it started working in the world,
would rouse mankind in every country,
even his own: go on and on and on,
continent after continent—Asia—Africa . . .

WOMAN

Or else he just forgot his slaves were men.

47

Archibald MacLeish

OLD MAN

That the mass of mankind are slaves—forgot it.

BLACK GIRL

Maybe he didn't think mankind are slaves:

Maybe he thought the masses of mankind are men.

JEFFERSON

"The mass of mankind," I wrote to the people of Washington, "the mass of mankind has not been born with saddles on their backs for a favored few, booted and spurred, ready to ride them by the grace of God . . ."

OLD MAN

He's mad. You don't make revolutions that way.

To make a revolution you convince mankind

they're licked, they're lost, they're mastered—finished.

"You have nothing to lose but your chains," you tell them.

GIRL

Maybe he meant a different revolution . . .

BLACK GIRL

Yes, maybe he did, a different revolution—

a revolution made by men for men

with men to do the ruling afterward,
not führers, not caudillos, commissars:
no pale Napoleon at the end to ride
those saddled backs with bloody spurs.
Free men, proud and gentle in their freedom!

(*brasses and drums off somewhere: the theme of the* Eroica)

OLD MAN

Then his revolution failed.
Look at the saddled, bridled, bleeding world
the revolutions of the century have left us.

GIRL

Or maybe not. Maybe the revolution he foresaw
went on and on and on and on—
to some parts sooner, others later . . .

BLACK GIRL

Maybe he meant that liberty is still to win—
is always still to win—is always liberty . . .

(*the brasses and drums louder and nearer*)

BULLHORN VOICE

Fall in! Take your places!

(*hurrying footsteps*)

Archibald MacLeish

V O I C E S

(*young, old, men, women*)

Mass of mankind . . .

The mass of mankind has not been born . . .

The mass of mankind has not been born
saddled and bridled . . .

                        a favored few
booted and spurred by the grace of God . . .

ready to ride by the grace of God . . .

by the grace of God . . .

                        by the grace of God . . .

(*the music*)

for the favored few who rule to ride
by the grace of God with a whip beside . . .

The mass of mankind has not been born
saddled and bridled for rulers to ride

but to govern themselves by the grace of God

and they will by the grace of God

                        they will!

By the grace of God they will!

                        They will!

(*the full* Eroica)

A D A M S

(*quiet voice*)

Thomas Jefferson still lives.

COLOPHON

The text of this book was set by Heritage Printers, Inc.,
in the Linotype version of Palatino, a type designed by
Hermann Zapf and aptly named for the Italian scribe. It is
a recent design, a product of the industrial age in many
respects, yet its formal classification in the families of
types would be in the Old Style category: a fitting combi-
nation for this book. The designer of the book is Gary Gore.